Personal Information

NAME

PHONE

CELL

EMAIL

STREET

CITY, STATE, ZIP

COUNTRY

Cornell Notes

Topic / Objective:	Class / Period:
	Date:

Essential Question:

At the top of every set of Cornell Notes, you should have the stated Essential Question. Many times your teacher will give it to you, but if they don't, you should be able to create one on your own.

Questions:	Notes:

Reduce & then Recite

- Create questions which elicit critical thinking, not 1 word answers
- Write questions directly across from the answers in your notes
- Leave a space or draw a pencil line separating questions

Record for Review

- Write headings and key words in colored pencil or pen
- Take sufficient notes with selective (not too much verbiage) & accurate paraphrasing
- Skip a line between ideas and topics
- Use bulleted lists and abbreviations
- Correctly sequence information
- Include diagrams or tables if needed for clarification or length

Summary:

When the lecture or meeting has finished, use this space section to summarize what was covered in the session, highlighting the most important points.

Cornell Notes

Topic / Objective:	Class / Period:
	Date:

Essential Question:

Questions:	Notes:

Summary:

Cornell Notes

Topic / Objective:	Class / Period:
	Date:

Essential Question:

Questions:	Notes:

Summary:

Cornell Notes

Topic / Objective:

Class / Period:

Date:

Essential Question:

Questions:

Notes:

Summary:

Cornell Notes

Topic / Objective:	Class / Period:
	Date:

Essential Question:

Questions:	Notes:

Summary:

Cornell Notes

Topic / Objective:	Class / Period:
	Date:

Essential Question:

Questions:	Notes:

Summary:

Cornell Notes

Topic / Objective:	Class / Period:
	Date:

Essential Question:

Questions:	Notes:

Summary:

Cornell Notes

Topic / Objective:	Class / Period:
	Date:

Essential Question:

Questions:	Notes:

Summary:

Cornell Notes

Topic / Objective:	Class / Period:
	Date:

Essential Question:

Questions:	Notes:

Summary:

Cornell Notes

Topic / Objective:	Class / Period:
	Date:

Essential Question:

Questions:	Notes:

Summary:

Cornell Notes

Topic / Objective:	Class / Period:
	Date:

Essential Question:

Questions:	Notes:

Summary:

Cornell Notes

Topic / Objective:

Class / Period:

Date:

Essential Question:

Questions:	Notes:

Summary:

Cornell Notes

Topic / Objective:	Class / Period:
	Date:

Essential Question:

Questions:	Notes:

Summary:

Cornell Notes

Topic / Objective:	Class / Period:
	Date:

Essential Question:

Questions:	Notes:

Summary:

Cornell Notes

Topic / Objective:	Class / Period:
	Date:

Essential Question:

Questions:	Notes:

Summary:

Cornell Notes

Topic / Objective:	Class / Period:
	Date:

Essential Question:

Questions:	Notes:

Summary:

Cornell Notes

Topic / Objective:	Class / Period:
	Date:

Essential Question:

Questions:	Notes:

Summary:

Cornell Notes

Topic / Objective:	Class / Period:
	Date:

Essential Question:

Questions:	Notes:

Summary:

Cornell Notes

Topic / Objective:	Class / Period:
	Date:

Essential Question:

Questions:	Notes:

Summary:

Cornell Notes

Topic / Objective:	Class / Period:
	Date:

Essential Question:

Questions:	Notes:

Summary:

Cornell Notes

Topic / Objective:	Class / Period:
	Date:

Essential Question:

Questions:	Notes:

Summary:

Cornell Notes

Topic / Objective:	Class / Period:
	Date:

Essential Question:

Questions: | **Notes:**

Summary:

Cornell Notes

Topic / Objective:	Class / Period:
	Date:

Essential Question:

Questions:	Notes:

Summary:

Cornell Notes

Topic / Objective:	Class / Period:
	Date:

Essential Question:

Questions:	Notes:

Summary:

Cornell Notes

Topic / Objective:

Class / Period:

Date:

Essential Question:

Questions:	Notes:

Summary:

Cornell Notes

Topic / Objective:	Class / Period:
	Date:

Essential Question:

Questions:	Notes:

Summary:

Cornell Notes

Topic / Objective:	Class / Period:
	Date:

Essential Question:

Questions:	Notes:

Summary:

Cornell Notes

Topic / Objective:	Class / Period:
	Date:

Essential Question:

Questions:	Notes:

Summary:

Cornell Notes

Topic / Objective:	Class / Period:
	Date:

Essential Question:

Questions:	Notes:

Summary:

Cornell Notes

Topic / Objective:	Class / Period:
	Date:

Essential Question:

Questions:	Notes:

Summary:

Cornell Notes

Topic / Objective:	Class / Period:
	Date:

Essential Question:

Questions:	Notes:

Summary:

Cornell Notes

Topic / Objective:	Class / Period:
	Date:

Essential Question:

Questions:	Notes:

Summary:

Cornell Notes

Topic / Objective:	Class / Period:
	Date:

Essential Question:

Questions:	Notes:

Summary:

Cornell Notes

Topic / Objective:	Class / Period:
	Date:

Essential Question:

Questions:	Notes:

Summary:

Cornell Notes

Topic / Objective:	Class / Period:
	Date:

Essential Question:

Questions:	Notes:

Summary:

Cornell Notes

Topic / Objective:	Class / Period:
	Date:

Essential Question:

Questions:	Notes:

Summary:

Cornell Notes

Topic / Objective:	Class / Period:
	Date:

Essential Question:

Questions:	Notes:

Summary:

Cornell Notes

Topic / Objective:	Class / Period:
	Date:

Essential Question:

Questions:	Notes:

Summary:

Cornell Notes

Topic / Objective:

Class / Period:

Date:

Essential Question:

Questions:	Notes:

Summary:

Cornell Notes

Topic / Objective:	Class / Period:
	Date:

Essential Question:

Questions:	Notes:

Summary:

Cornell Notes

Topic / Objective:	Class / Period:
	Date:

Essential Question:

Questions:	Notes:

Summary:

Cornell Notes

Topic / Objective:	Class / Period:
	Date:

Essential Question:

Questions:	Notes:

Summary:

Cornell Notes

Topic / Objective:

Class / Period:

Date:

Essential Question:

Questions:

Notes:

Summary:

Cornell Notes

Topic / Objective:	Class / Period:
	Date:

Essential Question:

Questions: | **Notes:**

Summary:

Cornell Notes

Topic / Objective:	Class / Period:
	Date:

Essential Question:

Questions:	Notes:

Summary:

Cornell Notes

Topic / Objective:	Class / Period:
	Date:

Essential Question:

Questions:	Notes:

Summary:

Cornell Notes

Topic / Objective:

Class / Period:

Date:

Essential Question:

Questions:	Notes:

Summary:

Cornell Notes

Topic / Objective:

Class / Period:

Date:

Essential Question:

Questions:	Notes:

Summary:

Cornell Notes

Topic / Objective:	Class / Period:
	Date:

Essential Question:

Questions:	Notes:

Summary:

Cornell Notes

Topic / Objective:	Class / Period:
	Date:

Essential Question:

Questions:	Notes:

Summary:

Cornell Notes

Topic / Objective:	Class / Period:
	Date:

Essential Question:

Questions:	Notes:

Summary:

Cornell Notes

Topic / Objective:

Class / Period:

Date:

Essential Question:

Questions:	Notes:

Summary:

Cornell Notes

Topic / Objective:	Class / Period:
	Date:

Essential Question:

Questions:	Notes:

Summary:

Cornell Notes

Topic / Objective:	Class / Period:
	Date:

Essential Question:

Questions:	Notes:

Summary:

Cornell Notes

Topic / Objective:	Class / Period:
	Date:

Essential Question:

Questions:	Notes:

Summary:

Cornell Notes

Topic / Objective:	Class / Period:
	Date:

Essential Question:

Questions:	Notes:

Summary:

Cornell Notes

Topic / Objective:	Class / Period:
	Date:

Essential Question:

Questions:	Notes:

Summary:

Cornell Notes

Topic / Objective:	Class / Period:
	Date:

Essential Question:

Questions:	Notes:

Summary:

Cornell Notes

Topic / Objective:	Class / Period:
	Date:

Essential Question:

Questions:	Notes:

Summary:

Cornell Notes

Topic / Objective:	Class / Period:
	Date:

Essential Question:

Questions:	Notes:

Summary:

Cornell Notes

Topic / Objective:

Class / Period:

Date:

Essential Question:

Questions:	Notes:

Summary:

Cornell Notes

Topic / Objective:	Class / Period:
	Date:

Essential Question:

Questions:	Notes:

Summary:

Cornell Notes

Topic / Objective:	Class / Period:
	Date:

Essential Question:

Questions:	Notes:

Summary:

Cornell Notes

Topic / Objective:	Class / Period:
	Date:

Essential Question:

Questions:	Notes:

Summary:

Cornell Notes

Topic / Objective:	Class / Period:
	Date:

Essential Question:

Questions:	Notes:

Summary:

Cornell Notes

Topic / Objective:	Class / Period:
	Date:

Essential Question:

Questions:	Notes:

Summary:

Cornell Notes

Topic / Objective:

Class / Period:

Date:

Essential Question:

Questions:

Notes:

Summary:

Cornell Notes

Topic / Objective:	Class / Period:
	Date:

Essential Question:

Questions:	Notes:

Summary:

Cornell Notes

Topic / Objective:	Class / Period:
	Date:

Essential Question:

Questions:	Notes:

Summary:

Cornell Notes

Topic / Objective:	Class / Period:
	Date:

Essential Question:

Questions:	Notes:

Summary:

Cornell Notes

Topic / Objective:	Class / Period:
	Date:

Essential Question:

Questions:	Notes:

Summary:

Cornell Notes

Topic / Objective:	Class / Period:
	Date:

Essential Question:

Questions:	Notes:

Summary:

Cornell Notes

Topic / Objective:	Class / Period:
	Date:

Essential Question:

Questions:	Notes:

Summary:

Cornell Notes

Topic / Objective:

Class / Period:

Date:

Essential Question:

Questions:	Notes:

Summary:

Cornell Notes

Topic / Objective:	Class / Period:
	Date:

Essential Question:

Questions:	Notes:

Summary:

Cornell Notes

Topic / Objective:	Class / Period:
	Date:

Essential Question:

Questions:	Notes:

Summary:

Cornell Notes

Topic / Objective:	Class / Period:
	Date:

Essential Question:

Questions:	**Notes:**

Summary:

Cornell Notes

Topic / Objective:

Class / Period:

Date:

Essential Question:

Questions:	Notes:

Summary:

Cornell Notes

Topic / Objective:	Class / Period:
	Date:

Essential Question:

Questions:	Notes:

Summary:

Cornell Notes

Topic / Objective:	Class / Period:
	Date:

Essential Question:

Questions:	Notes:

Summary:

Cornell Notes

Topic / Objective:	Class / Period:
	Date:

Essential Question:

Questions:	Notes:

Summary:

Cornell Notes

Topic / Objective:	Class / Period:
	Date:

Essential Question:

Questions:	Notes:

Summary:

Cornell Notes

Topic / Objective:

Class / Period:

Date:

Essential Question:

Questions:

Notes:

Summary:

Cornell Notes

Topic / Objective:	Class / Period:
	Date:

Essential Question:

Questions:	Notes:

Summary:

Cornell Notes

Topic / Objective:	Class / Period:
	Date:

Essential Question:

Questions:	Notes:

Summary:

Cornell Notes

Topic / Objective:	Class / Period:
	Date:

Essential Question:

Questions:	Notes:

Summary:

Cornell Notes

Topic / Objective:	Class / Period:
	Date:

Essential Question:

Questions:	Notes:

Summary:

Cornell Notes

Topic / Objective:	Class / Period:
	Date:

Essential Question:

Questions:	Notes:

Summary:

Cornell Notes

Topic / Objective:	Class / Period:
	Date:

Essential Question:

Questions:	Notes:

Summary:

Cornell Notes

Topic / Objective:

Class / Period:

Date:

Essential Question:

Questions:	Notes:

Summary:

Cornell Notes

Topic / Objective:	Class / Period:
	Date:

Essential Question:

Questions:	Notes:

Summary:

Cornell Notes

Topic / Objective:	Class / Period:
	Date:

Essential Question:

Questions:	Notes:

Summary:

Cornell Notes

Topic / Objective:	Class / Period:
	Date:

Essential Question:

Questions:	Notes:

Summary:

Cornell Notes

Topic / Objective:

Class / Period:

Date:

Essential Question:

Questions:	Notes:

Summary:

Cornell Notes

Topic / Objective:	Class / Period:
	Date:

Essential Question:

Questions:	Notes:

Summary:

Cornell Notes

Topic / Objective:	Class / Period:
	Date:

Essential Question:

Questions:	Notes:

Summary:

Cornell Notes

Topic / Objective:	Class / Period:
	Date:

Essential Question:

Questions:	Notes:

Summary:

Cornell Notes

Topic / Objective:	Class / Period:
	Date:

Essential Question:

Questions:	Notes:

Summary:

Cornell Notes

Topic / Objective:

Class / Period:

Date:

Essential Question:

Questions:	Notes:

Summary:

Cornell Notes

Topic / Objective:	Class / Period:
	Date:

Essential Question:

Questions:	Notes:

Summary:

Cornell Notes

Topic / Objective:	Class / Period:
	Date:

Essential Question:

Questions:	Notes:

Summary:

Cornell Notes

Topic / Objective:	Class / Period:
	Date:

Essential Question:

Questions:	Notes:

Summary:

Cornell Notes

Topic / Objective:	Class / Period:
	Date:

Essential Question:

Questions:	Notes:

Summary:

Cornell Notes

Topic / Objective:	Class / Period:
	Date:

Essential Question:

Questions:	Notes:

Summary:

Cornell Notes

Topic / Objective:	Class / Period:
	Date:

Essential Question:

Questions:	Notes:

Summary:

Cornell Notes

Topic / Objective:	Class / Period:
	Date:

Essential Question:

Questions:	Notes:

Summary:

Cornell Notes

Topic / Objective:	Class / Period:
	Date:

Essential Question:

Questions:	Notes:

Summary:

Cornell Notes

Topic / Objective:

Class / Period:

Date:

Essential Question:

Questions:	Notes:

Summary:

Cornell Notes

Topic / Objective:	Class / Period:
	Date:

Essential Question:

Questions:	Notes:

Summary:

Cornell Notes

Topic / Objective:

Class / Period:

Date:

Essential Question:

Questions:	Notes:

Summary:

Cornell Notes

Topic / Objective:	Class / Period:
	Date:

Essential Question:

Questions:	Notes:

Summary:

Cornell Notes

Topic / Objective:	Class / Period:
	Date:

Essential Question:

Questions:	Notes:

Summary:

Cornell Notes

Topic / Objective:	Class / Period:
	Date:

Essential Question:

Questions:	Notes:

Summary:

Cornell Notes

Topic / Objective:	Class / Period:
	Date:

Essential Question:

Questions:	Notes:

Summary:

Cornell Notes

Topic / Objective:

Class / Period:

Date:

Essential Question:

Questions:	Notes:

Summary:

Cornell Notes

Topic / Objective:	Class / Period:
	Date:

Essential Question:

Questions:	Notes:

Summary:

Cornell Notes

Topic / Objective:

Class / Period:

Date:

Essential Question:

Questions:	Notes:

Summary:

Cornell Notes

Topic / Objective:

Class / Period:

Date:

Essential Question:

Questions:	Notes:

Summary:

Cornell Notes

Topic / Objective:	Class / Period:
	Date:

Essential Question:

Questions:	Notes:

Summary:

Cornell Notes

Topic / Objective:

Class / Period:

Date:

Essential Question:

Questions:	Notes:

Summary:

Cornell Notes

Topic / Objective:	Class / Period:
	Date:

Essential Question:

Questions:	Notes:

Summary:

Made in the USA
Monee, IL
07 September 2022